D1144157

HOW TO DRAW TREES AND WOODLAND

Mark Bergin

BOOK  HOUSE

SALARIYA

© The Salariya Book Company Ltd MMVIII
All rights reserved. No part of this book may be reproduced, stored in a retrieval system or transmitted in any form or by any means, electronic, mechanical, photocopying, recording or otherwise, without the written permission of the copyright owner.

Published in Great Britain in MMVIII by
Book House, an imprint of
The Salariya Book Company Ltd
25 Marlborough Place, Brighton BN1 1UB

3 5 7 9 8 6 4

Please visit our website at **www.salariya.com**
for **free** electronic versions of:
You Wouldn't Want to Be an Egyptian Mummy!
You Wouldn't Want to Be a Roman Gladiator!
Avoid Joining Shackleton's Polar Expedition!
Avoid Sailing on a 19th-Century Whaling Ship!

Author: Mark Bergin was born in Hastings, England, in 1961. He studied at Eastbourne College of Art and his specialities include historical reconstructions, aviation and maritime subjects. He lives in Bexhill-on-Sea with his wife and three children.

Editors: Rob Walker, Stephen Haynes

PB ISBN: 978-1-906370-32-9

A CIP catalogue record for this book is available from the British Library.

Printed and bound in China.
Printed on paper from sustainable sources.
Reprinted in MMXIII.

WARNING: Fixatives should be used only under adult supervision.

PAPER FROM SUSTAINABLE FORESTS

Contents

Making a start

Learning to draw is about looking and seeing. Keep practising, and get to know your subject. Use a sketchbook to make quick sketches. Start by doodling, and experiment with shapes and patterns. There are many ways to draw; this book shows one method. Visit art galleries, look at artists' drawings, see how friends draw, but above all, find your own way.

Remember that practice makes perfect. If it looks wrong, start again. Keep working at it – the more you draw, the more you will learn.

Wax crayon
Ballpoint pen
Felt–tip
Ink (pen
and sponge)

Perspective

If you look at any object from different viewpoints, you will see that the part that is closest to you looks larger, and the part furthest away from you looks smaller. Drawing in perspective is a way of creating a feeling of space – of showing three dimensions on a flat surface.

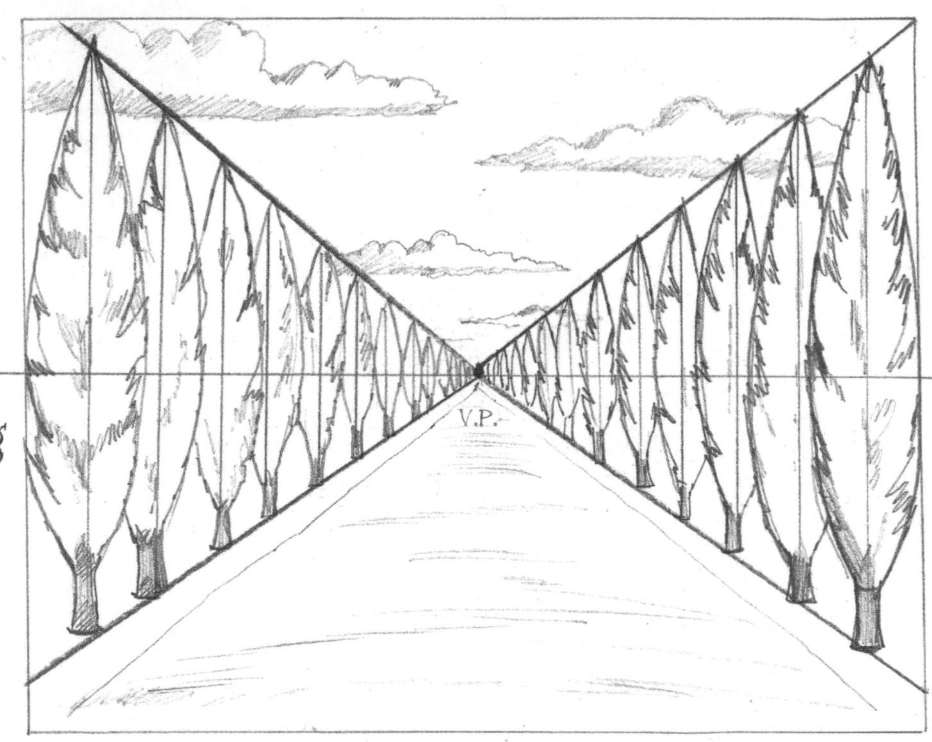

The vanishing point (V.P.) is the place in a perspective drawing where parallel lines appear to meet. Objects closer to the vanishing point appear further away.

The position of the vanishing point depends on the viewer's eye level. Sometimes a low viewpoint can give your drawing added drama.

One-point perspective drawing

One-point perspective uses one vanishing point: all parallel lines drawn through the picture come together at a single point.

In the drawings on this page, the vanishing point is outside the picture.

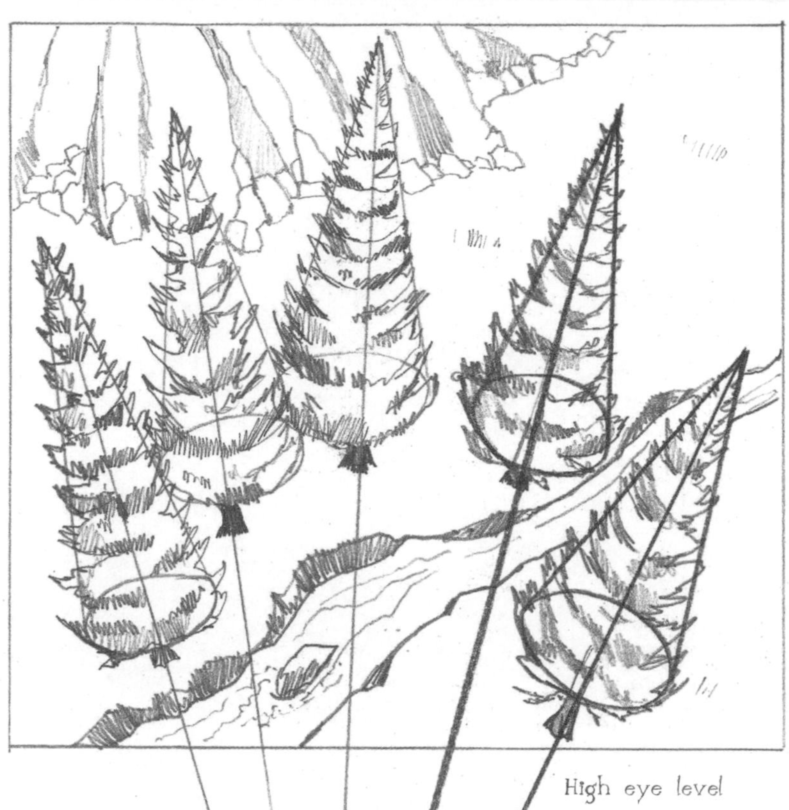

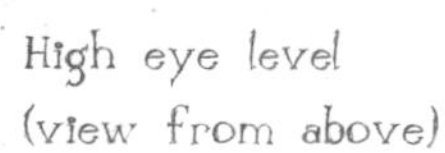
High eye level
(view from above)

V.P.

Low eye level
(view from below)

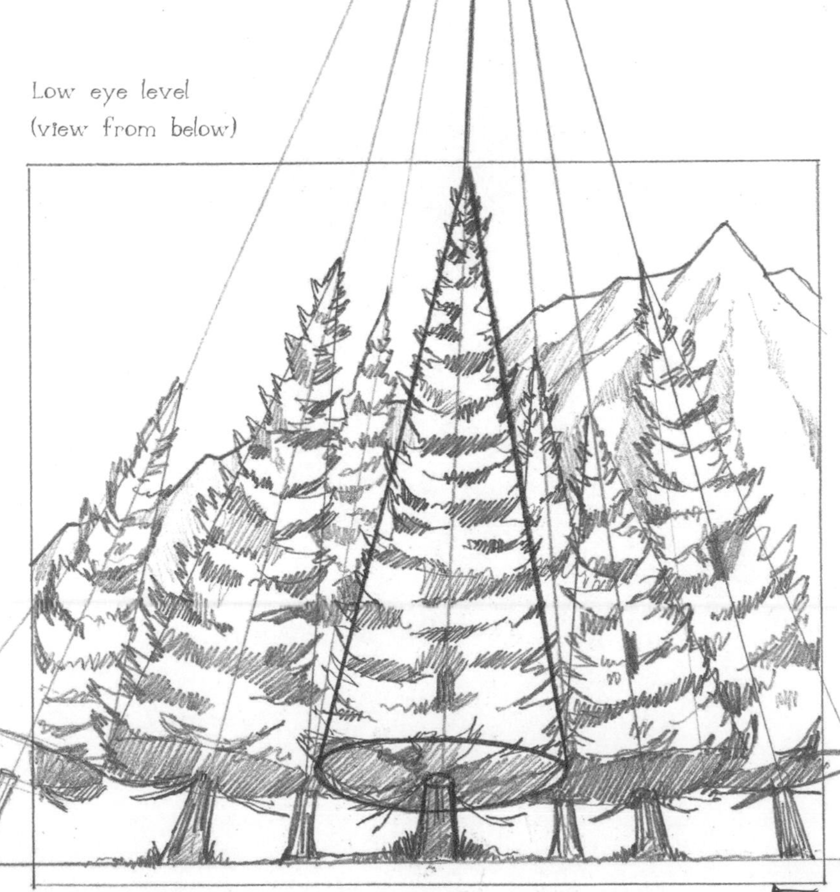

In one-point perspective, placing the vanishing point above the picture gives you a low viewpoint. This makes the trees seem to tower over you. Placing the vanishing point below the picture gives you a high viewpoint, as if you were looking down from a helicopter.

V.P. = vanishing point

Materials

Try using different types of drawing papers and materials. Experiment with charcoal, wax crayons and pastels. All pens, from felt–tips to ballpoints, will make interesting marks. Try drawing with pen and ink on wet paper.

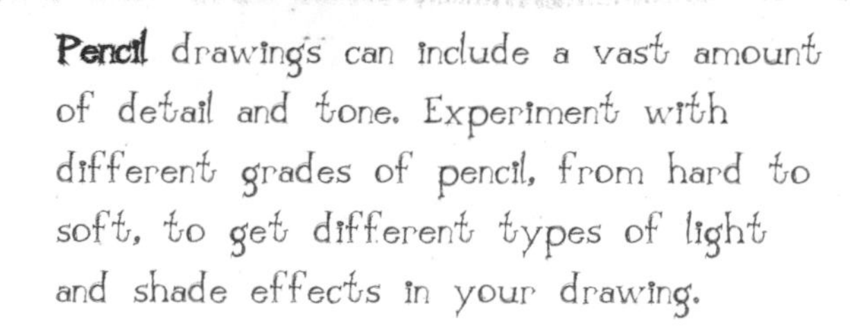

Pencil drawings can include a vast amount of detail and tone. Experiment with different grades of pencil, from hard to soft, to get different types of light and shade effects in your drawing.

Soft pencil and charcoal will smudge unless they are sprayed with fixative. **Always ask an adult to do this for you.**

Felt–tips come in a range of line widths. The wider pens are good for filling in large areas of flat tone.

Lines drawn in **ink** cannot be erased, so keep your ink drawings sketchy and less rigid. Don't worry about mistakes, as these can be lost in the drawing as it develops.

Adding areas of different tone to a drawing with an ink pen can be difficult. Use solid ink for the very darkest areas and cross-hatching (straight lines criss-crossing each other) for dark tones. Use hatching (straight lines running parallel to each other) for midtones, and keep the lightest areas empty.

Ink silhouette

Remember, the best equipment and materials will not necessarily make the best drawing – practice will!

Using photos

Drawing from photographs of real trees can help you develop your drawing skills and your eye for detail.

Drawing from photographs

Make a tracing of a photograph and draw a grid of squares over it.

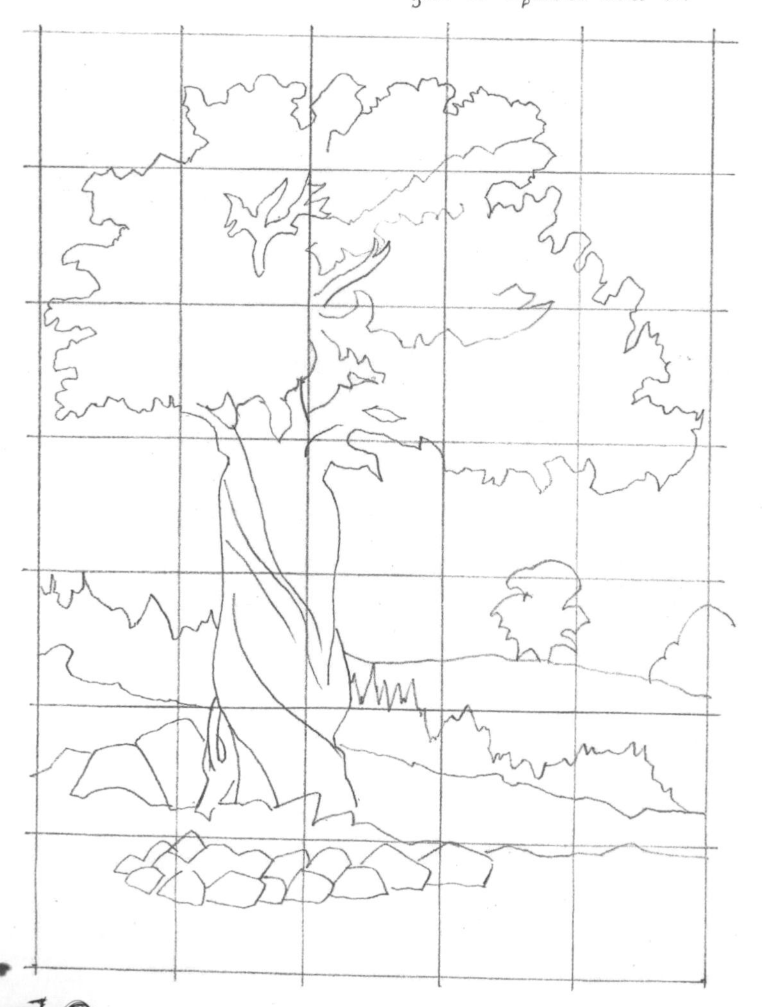

Now draw another grid on your drawing paper, enlarging or reducing the squares but keeping the same proportions. You can now copy the shapes from each square of your tracing to your drawing paper, using the grid as a guide.

To make your drawing look three-dimensional, decide which side the light is coming from, and put in areas of shadow on the opposite side.

Sketch in an overall tone and add ground texture to create interest and a sense of movement. Pay attention to the position of your drawing on the paper; this is called composition.

Sketching

You can't always rely on your memory, so you have to look around and find real-life things you want to draw. Using a sketchbook is one of the best ways to build up drawing skills. Learn to observe objects: see how they move, how they are made and how they work. What you draw should be what you have seen. Since the 15th century, artists have used sketchbooks to record their ideas and drawings.

Trees are everywhere, and they come in many different forms. Each one presents you with a new drawing challenge.

Sketching the details of the tree's leaves can help you understand how to draw the tree as a whole.

At any local park you will be able to look at trees from all sorts of angles.

The trees may even have labels to tell you what species they are. If they do, make a note of this on your sketch.

A quick sketch can often be as informative as a careful drawing that has taken many hours.

Landscapes

The environment can affect the shape of trees in the natural landscape. For example, a tree can become windswept if it is growing by itself and is regularly exposed to the wind. The landscape also provides an interesting backdrop for your drawing of a tree.

This drawing of a tree has been made more interesting by including the river and the reflections of the trees in the water.

Some trees have an interesting shape due to the prevailing winds. As this tree has grown, the strong winds have forced it to lean to one side.

These trees have been planted close together, which has made them grow tall and narrow as they reach up towards the sunlight.

Deciduous trees lose all of their leaves for part of the year. Here is an oak tree with and without its foliage. Each version presents different drawing challenges.

Roots and stumps

Drawing tree roots and stumps will improve your drawing skills by focusing your eye on shape and detail. The highlights and shadows on the roots and the shapes that are formed by them create interesting designs.

The base of this tree has split and grown in different directions.

Oddly shaped trees can make lively drawings.

The roots of this tree are exposed. Their twisted forms create a wonderfully intricate design.

Old tree stumps can make very interesting drawing projects. Broken and splintered stumps with fungi and other plant life growing on them can be quite fascinating. See how much detail you can capture.

Lombardy poplar

The Lombardy poplar was first grown in Lombardy, in northern Italy. The tree is tall and narrow, with a pointed shape. These trees are seen all over the Mediterranean region and are well adapted to hot, dry summers.

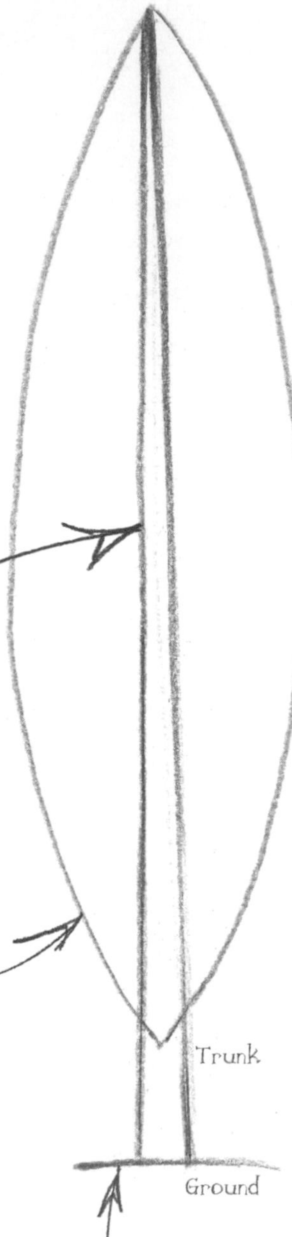

Sketch in the tree trunk with two straight lines.

Draw in the main shape of the tree with two curved lines meeting at either end. These are construction lines that can be rubbed out when the drawing is finished.

Trunk

Ground

Add a line for the ground.

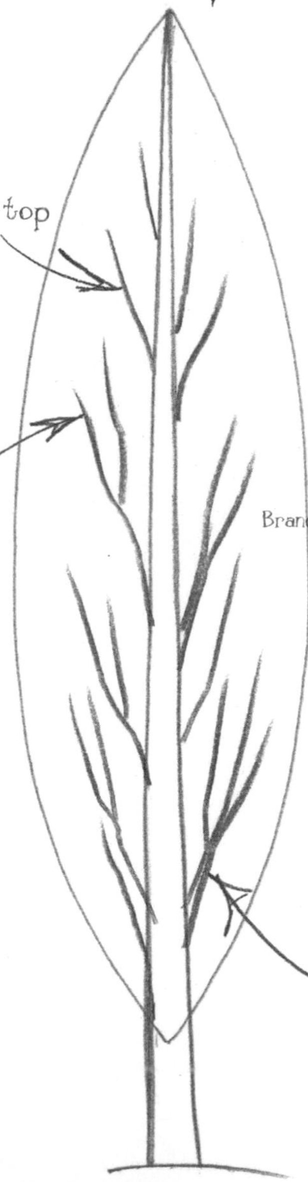

Sketch in short upward lines for branches near the top of the tree.

Most branches have several smaller branches sprouting out from them.

Branches

The branches at the base of the tree are longer than those at the top.

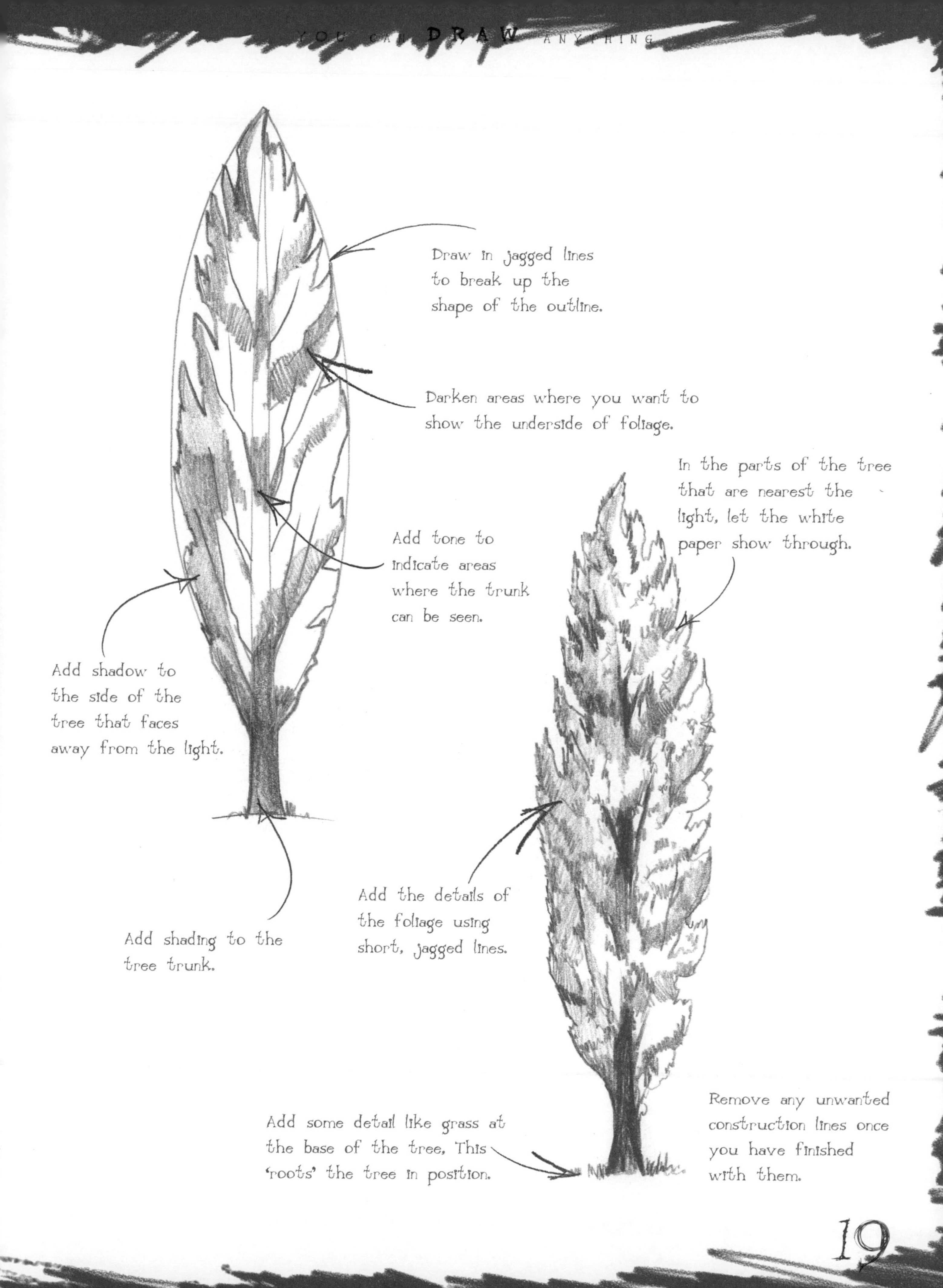
Draw in jagged lines
to break up the
shape of the outline.
Darken areas where you want to
show the underside of foliage.
Add tone to
indicate areas
where the trunk
can be seen.
Add shadow to
the side of the
tree that faces
away from the light.
Add shading to the
tree trunk.
In the parts of the tree
that are nearest the
light, let the white
paper show through.
Add the details of
the foliage using
short, jagged lines.
Add some detail like grass at
the base of the tree. This
'roots' the tree in position.
Remove any unwanted
construction lines once
you have finished
with them.

Fir tree

Fir trees can be found through much of North and Central America, Europe, Asia and North Africa. They naturally occur on mountain ranges.

Construction lines

Sketching construction lines helps you to keep the shape of your drawing in proportion.

Sketch in the details of the foliage using jagged lines.

The tip of each branch should point upwards.

The top part of each branch is nearer the light, so keep the foliage lighter here.

Darken areas where the trunk shows through.

The bottom of the tree trunk should curve outwards.

Use short, jagged lines to draw in the texture of the foliage.

The darkest tone should be on the trunk of the tree.

Add grass to the ground around the base of the tree.

Remove any unwanted construction lines.

Palm tree

Palm trees are abundant throughout the tropical regions of the world. They are found in almost every type of habitat in the tropics.

Coconuts

Add three overlapping ovals at the top of the trunk for coconuts.

Draw two gently curved lines for the tree trunk.

Trunk

Ground

Draw in a line for the ground.

Leaves

Draw curved lines joining at the tips for the large branches and leaves.

The branches should start at the top of the trunk and fan outwards.

Using a mirror

You can often see mistakes more easily by looking at the drawing in reverse, using a mirror.

Both sides of the top two branches are visible, so draw the fringed edges on both sides.
Add short straight lines to the lower edge of the foliage to create a fringed edge.
Add jagged lines to complete the detail of the foliage.
Add shading to the underside of the coconuts and beneath them.
Sketch curved lines across the tree trunk.
Add tone to the leaves.
Add detail to the ground at the foot of the tree.
Complete the detail on the trunk.
Add more shading to areas that face away from the light.
Complete the detail at the foot of the tree.
Remove any unwanted construction lines.

Oak tree

The oak tree can be found in the northern hemisphere. The fruit of the oak tree is easy to recognise — it is a nut called an acorn that grows in a little cup.

Draw a series of curved lines for the trunk and main branches.

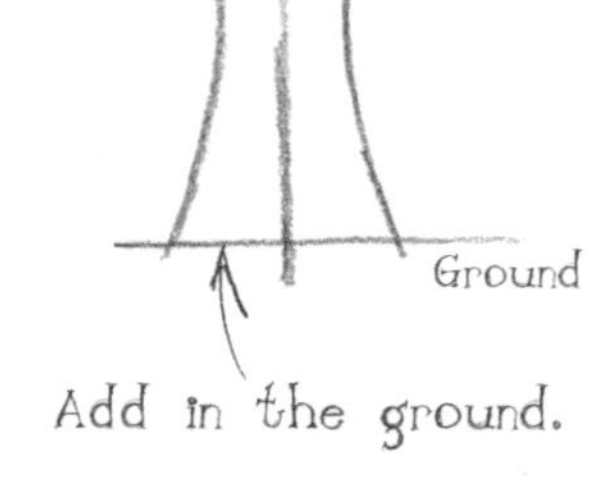

Add in the ground.

Draw in a large circular shape with slanting lines at the base to show the tree's shape.

Add more lines to each branch to create smaller branches.

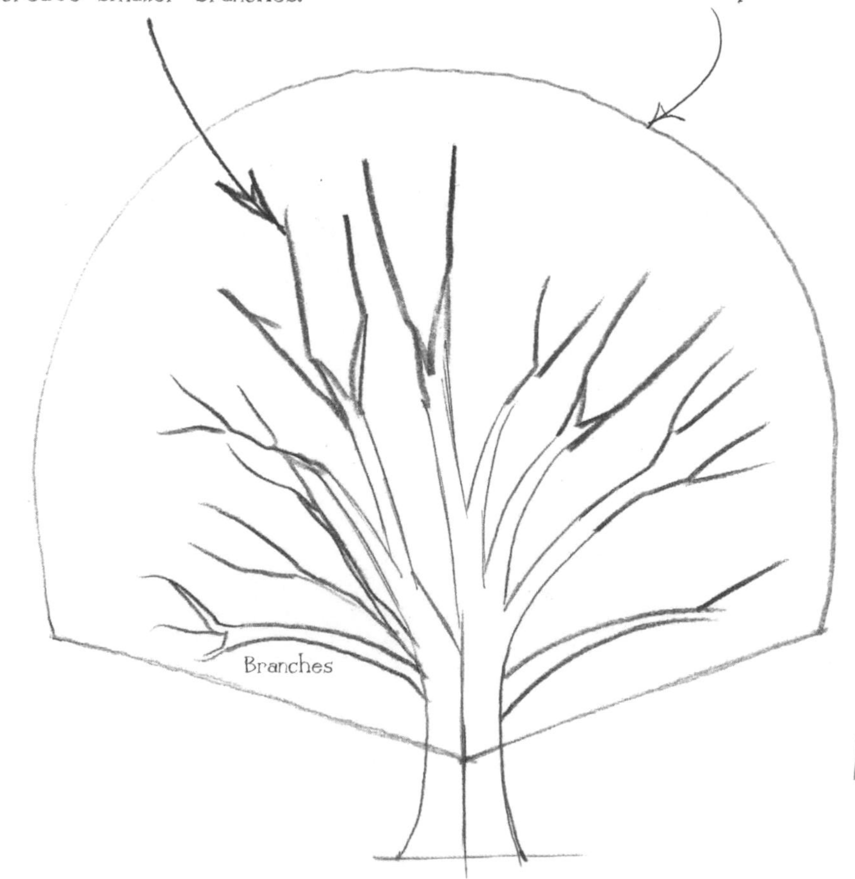

Negative space

Look at the space around the drawing (negative space) to help check the proportions and shape of your drawing.

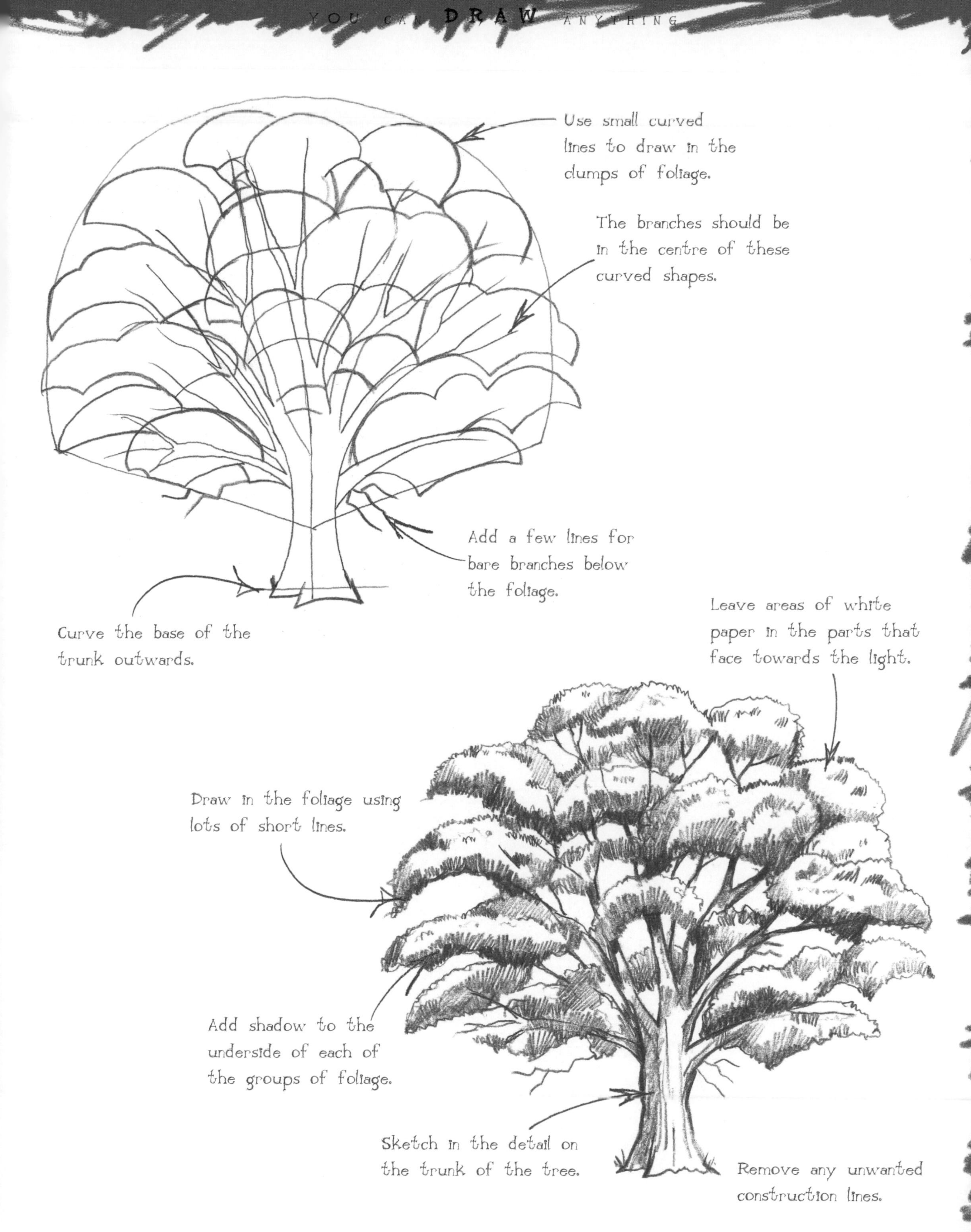
Use small curved lines to draw in the clumps of foliage.
The branches should be in the centre of these curved shapes.
Add a few lines for bare branches below the foliage.
Curve the base of the trunk outwards.
Leave areas of white paper in the parts that face towards the light.
Draw in the foliage using lots of short lines.
Add shadow to the underside of each of the groups of foliage.
Sketch in the detail on the trunk of the tree.
Remove any unwanted construction lines.

Baobab tree

The baobab is found in Africa and Australia. It is also known as the upside-down tree. There are eight species of baobab tree: six are found on the island of Madagascar, one in mainland Africa and one in Australia.

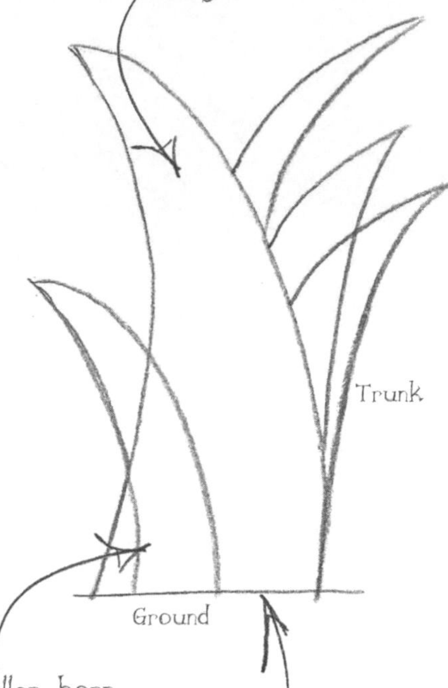

Draw in construction lines for the foliage using curved lines.
Add smaller branches and twigs.
The foliage on this tree hangs downwards.
Suggest the bark of the tree by sketching short lines across the trunk.
Add tone to leaves to give the drawing more impact.
The leaves on this tree are very small and can be drawn in using dots.
Add more tone and detail to the bark of the tree.
Remove any unwanted construction lines.
Choose the direction of the light source and add shading to the tree trunk and branches.
Draw in detail around the base of the trunk.

Giant sequoia tree

The giant sequoia is the world's tallest tree, reaching up to 115.5 metres. The base of its trunk can be 7 metres in diameter. Its bark is not hard, but very thick, soft and fibrous. The tree has bright reddish wood – hence it is commonly known as 'giant redwood'.

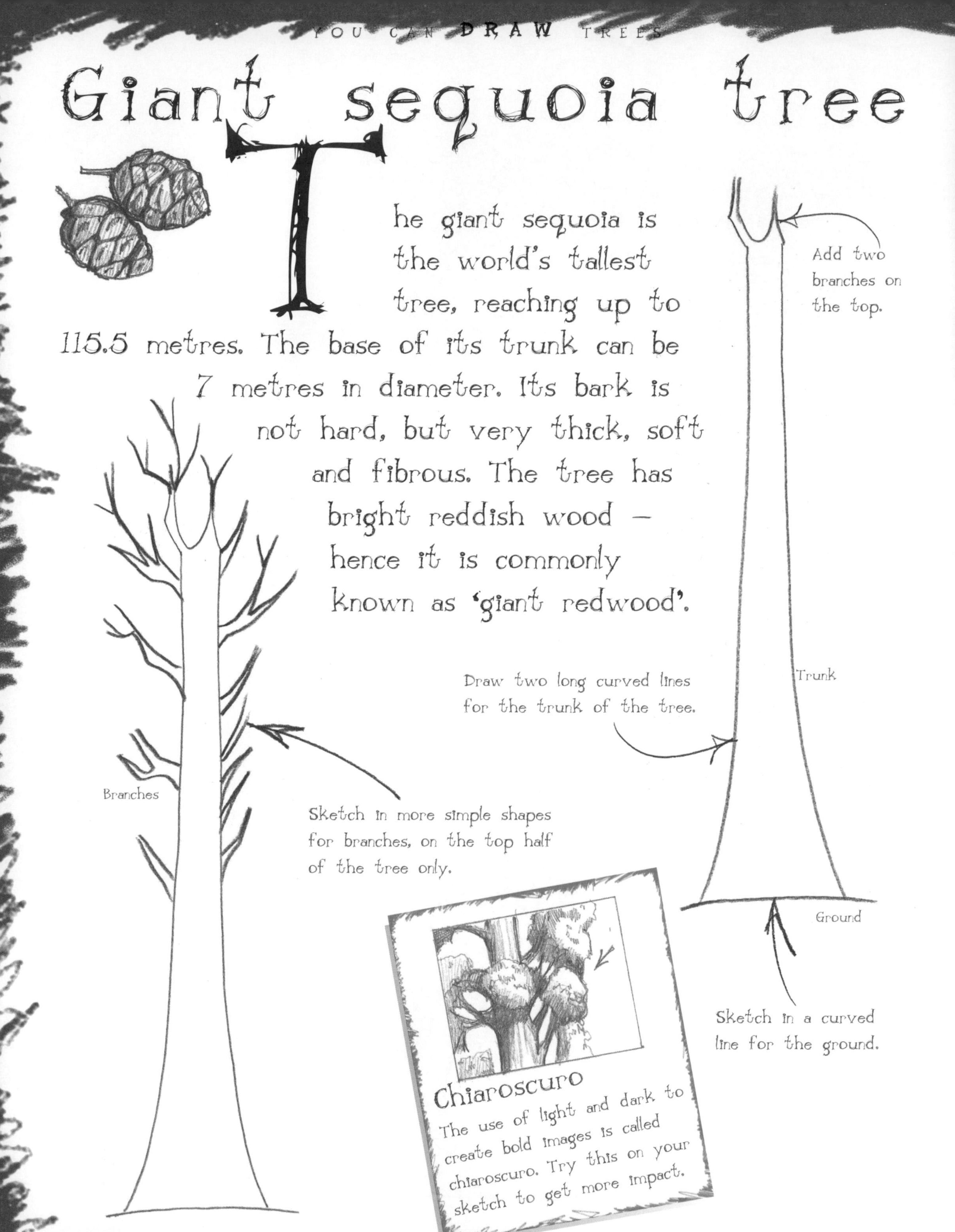

Chiaroscuro

The use of light and dark to create bold images is called chiaroscuro. Try this on your sketch to get more impact.

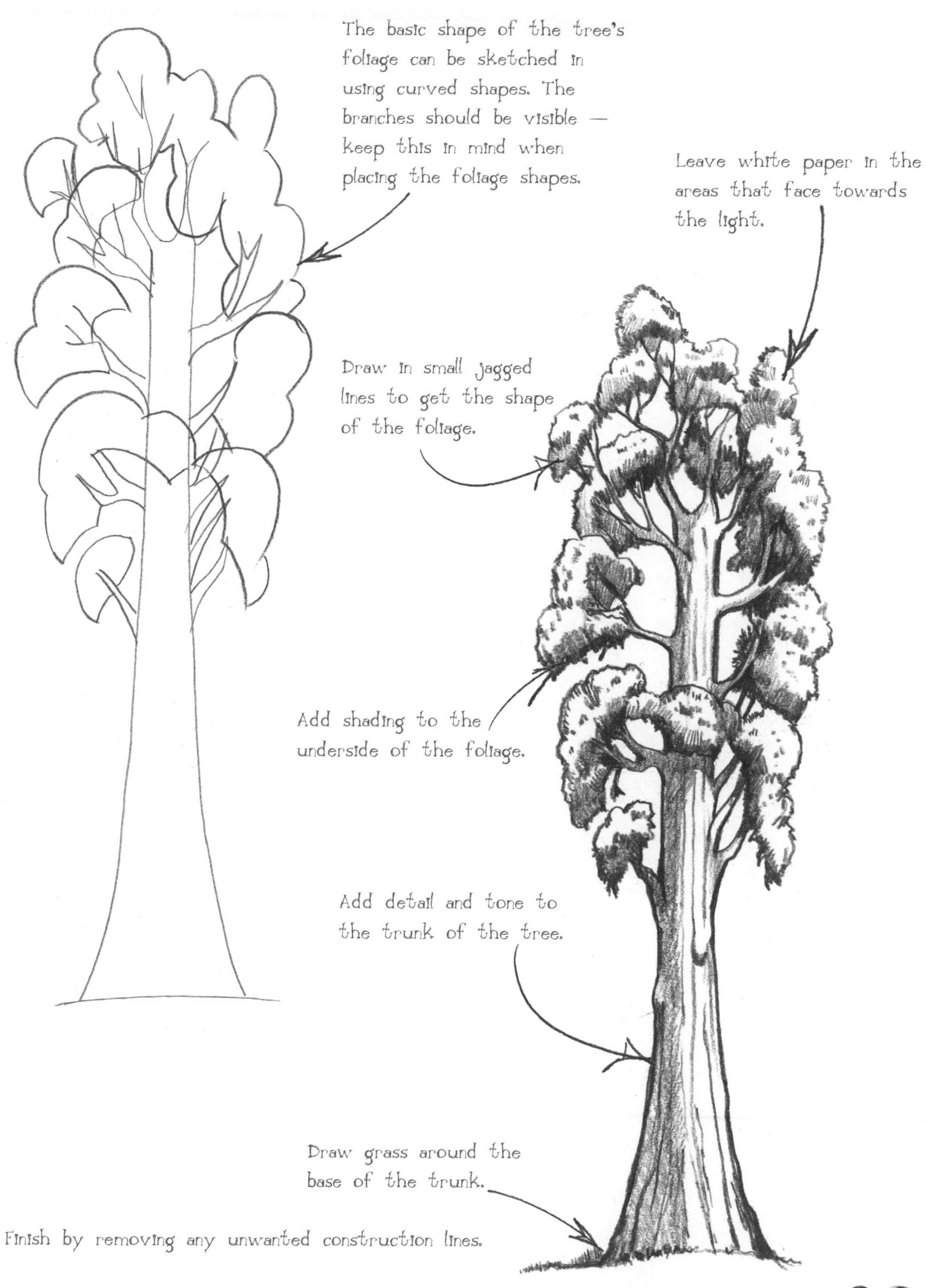

Finish by removing any unwanted construction lines.

Willow tree

The weeping willow is a very well-known ornamental tree. Often they are planted by rivers and lakes, as they do well close to water. The weeping willow is derived from the hybridisation (cross-breeding) of the Chinese Peking willow and the European white willow.

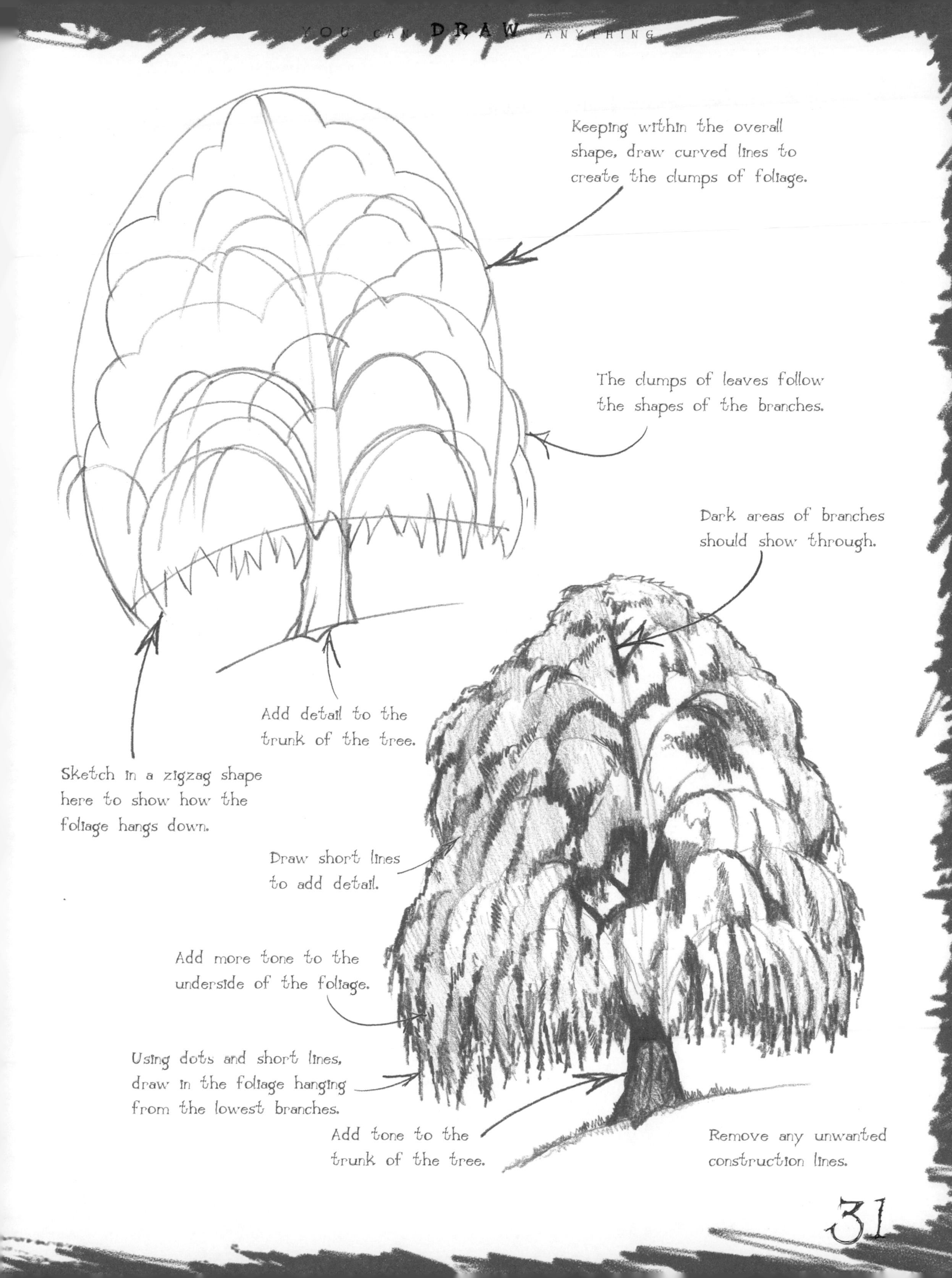
Keeping within the overall shape, draw curved lines to create the clumps of foliage.
The clumps of leaves follow the shapes of the branches.
Dark areas of branches should show through.
Add detail to the trunk of the tree.
Sketch in a zigzag shape here to show how the foliage hangs down.
Draw short lines to add detail.
Add more tone to the underside of the foliage.
Using dots and short lines, draw in the foliage hanging from the lowest branches.
Add tone to the trunk of the tree.
Remove any unwanted construction lines.

Glossary

Chiaroscuro The use of light and dark in a drawing.

Composition The positioning of a picture on the drawing paper.

Construction lines Structural lines used in the early stages of a drawing, and usually erased later.

Cross-hatching A series of criss-cross lines used to add shade to a drawing.

Fixative A type of resin used to spray over a finished drawing to prevent smudging. **It should only be used by an adult.**

Hatching A series of parallel lines used to add shade to a drawing.

Light source The direction from which the light seems to come in a drawing.

Negative space The space around and between the parts of a drawing.

Proportion The correct relationship of scale between the parts of a drawing.

Reference Photographs or other images used to help produce a drawing, if drawing from life is not possible.

Three-dimensional Having an effect of depth, so as to look lifelike or real.

Vanishing point The place in a perspective drawing where parallel lines appear to meet.

Index